Growing Your Love After The "I Do's" God's Way

Dr. Shameka Mack Sanders

© 2017 Dr. Shameka Mack Sanders
All rights reserved.

ISBN: 0998910201

ISBN 13: 9780998910208

Library of Congress Control Number: 2017905613

Sanders Publications LLC

With unconditional love, I dedicate this book to my best friend and praying partner, my husband, Clifton. Your faith patience and love has truly been a catalyst for rebuilding our marriage.

Contents

God's Plan Not Mine 15

The Wedding Day 25

Fake It Till You Make It or NOT 31

Enough Is Enough 51

The Truth Heals 63

Loving Your Spouse 75

Growing Your Love God's Way 83

Tips For Growing Your Love God's Way 89

Acknowledgments

I'll be the first to say that a happy and healthy marriage takes hard work—hard work from both you and your spouse. That being said, I'd like to thank my husband of nine years, Clifton, who made the choice to fight with me and not against me for our marriage. Yes, there were times when we both wanted to walk away, but we did not do it. It was Clifton's choice to walk by faith that helped me realize the importance of building a better relationship with God. It was Clifton, who showed me that marriage is not all about *my* wants, plans, and desires; rather, it is about "us" and *our* wants, plans, and desires. And, when I did not love myself, and felt like I was in this marriage by myself, it was Clifton, who reminded me that I was not alone, and for that I am forever grateful.

Without the spiritual guidance of Bishop Charles and Pastor Marion Dudley, Clifton and I would not be where we are today. Over the years, Bishop and Pastor Dudley became our spiritual parents. More specifically, they helped us realize our shortcomings, and taught us how to apply the Word of God to our marriage in a way that is not based on tradition and religion, but purely on the principles of God. Truth-be-told, it is always great to have people around you, who want you to succeed in every area of your life. Bishop and Pastor Dudley were those people for me. So, when I did things that were not helping my marriage improve, these two individuals pulled me back into God's light. And, truthfully, I needed that because even though I was trying to "better" my marriage, at times, I still found myself venturing towards bad habits and decision-making tendencies.

Foreword

Dr. Shameka Sanders and her husband, Clifton, were members at my church, while Clifton served in the United States Marine Corps. This couple sought spiritual counseling, and attended marriage-focused classes and seminars to improve and strengthen their relationship. Marriage and military service can lead to stagnation in a relationship, if the people involved do not work to grow their love.

Thankfully, Shameka and Clifton have always been willing and eager to learn and follow God's way. According to the National Survey of Family Growth, approximately 40% of marriages end in divorce, which highlights how challenging marriage can be when both partners are not fully committed to God's plan for marriage. This book is a blessing because it openly and honestly addresses some of the reasons why marriages fail and offers valuable suggestions on improving your chances of having a happy, healthy, and blessed union.

Because Shameka and Clifton are God-fearing, purpose-driven individuals, they have been able to develop a new, stronger foundation at which to base their marital union. Determined and unwavering, this couple has set out to grow their love in God's way! And, as a result of this life-altering decision, their relationship has changed for the better.

The transparent approach highlighted in this book helps struggling couples tackle and conquer marital issues with eleven simple and effective - but often overlooked principles.

These principles include:

Purposeful Happiness, Love and Respect, Change, Appreciation, Investment, Listening, Handling Conflict, Christ Centeredness, Financial Matters, and Intimacy and Privacy.

Shameka and Clifton are living proof that love can grow after the "I do's," especially when God's way is introduced into the relationship. This book will teach couples that the ultimate success of their marriage hinges on respect and equal contributions. I have no doubt that this book will change how the world views marriage.

I am committed to recommending *"Growing Your Love After The 'I Do's' God's Way,"* to every couple I pastor, mentor, or counsel.

Thank you, Shameka! Pastor Marion and I are most proud to call you a Daughter in the Faith!

Bishop Charles T. Dudley
Senior Pastor
New Beginnings Ministry of Faith
Havelock, North Carolina

God's Plan Not Mine

Marriage is more than a ceremony. It is the joining of two flawed individuals together, so they can become one. God's intention for us has always been to honor the marital union (Hebrews 13:4). God designed marriage with the ultimate purpose of reflecting His image (Genesis 2:18–24). Therefore, when the image of God is reflected in your marriage, you accept and receive your spouse, as God's *perfect* gift to you. In the same way that Eve, created differently from God's other creations, was a unique gift to Adam, your spouse is God's unique gift to you.

Give honor to marriage, and remain faithful to one another in marriage. (Hebrews 13:4 [NLT])

And the LORD God said, It is not good that the man should be alone; I will make him an help meet for him. And out of the ground the LORD God formed every beast of the field, and every fowl of the air; and brought them unto Adam to see what he would call them: and whatsoever Adam called every living creature, that was the name thereof. And Adam gave names to all cattle, and to the fowl of the air, and to every beast of the field; but for Adam there was not found an help meet for him. And the LORD God caused a deep sleep to fall upon Adam, and he slept: and he took one of his ribs, and closed up the flesh instead

> *thereof; And the rib, which the LORD God had taken from man, made he a woman, and brought her unto the man. And Adam said, This is now bone of my bones, and flesh of my flesh: she shall be called Woman, because she was taken out of Man. Therefore shall a man leave his father and his mother, and shall cleave unto his wife: and they shall be one flesh. (Genesis 2:18–24 [KJV])*

People choose marriage for many different reasons, yet, I am convinced that some divorce because they truly underestimate the amount of work it takes to make a marriage work. *Why?* Well, the answer is simple - we are selfish beings. In other words, it is not uncommon to say, "What about *me?*" or "What about the things *I* want to do?" or "What about what *I* need?" At the end of the day, however, it is necessary to understand that marriage is not all about *you* and *your* happiness, *your* fulfillment, or *your* entitlement. Rather, it's about overcoming issues *together*, serving each other, and, most importantly, serving God.

Understanding God's plan for my marriage was necessary, if Clifton and I were going to build a happy, healthy marriage. God created the marriage relationship with Adam and Eve, and I'm positive He never wanted us to give up when things became difficult (or even extremely difficult). In other words, He never intended for us to separate or divorce simply because we faced challenges in our relationships. And, even though there are circumstances when divorce is necessary, most of the time, divorces are both unnecessary and avoidable. The importance of this sentiment is underscored in Matthew 19:6 and Malachi 2:13–16.

Since they are no longer two but one, let no one split apart what God has joined together. (Matthew 19:6 [NLT])

Here is another thing you do. You cover the Lord's altar with tears, weeping and groaning because he pays no attention to

> *your offerings and doesn't accept them with pleasure. You cry out, "Why doesn't the Lord accept my worship?" I'll tell you why! Because the Lord witnessed the vows you and your wife made when you were young. But you have been unfaithful to her, though she remained your faithful partner, the wife of your marriage vows. Didn't the Lord make you one with your wife? In body and spirit you are his. And what does he want? Godly children from your union. So guard your heart; remain loyal to the wife of your youth. "For I hate divorce!" says the Lord, the God of Israel. "To divorce your wife is to overwhelm her with cruelty," says the Lord of Heaven's Armies. "So guard your heart; do not be unfaithful to your wife." (Malachi 2:13–16 [NLT])*

I had to accept that the ultimate purpose for marriage is to reflect God's image. And, God's ordained plan is to provide the world with a picture of His love. It is important to understand that marriage is a sacred union that helps us eliminate solitude, establish families, and raise children. As a married person, it is important to grow and resolve any issues with your spouse.

Furthermore, it was extremely important for me to receive my spouse daily, as God's special gift to me. *Did I have a hard time coming to this conclusion?* Absolutely, but I was willing to take the risk and work through the hurt and pain that had accumulated over the years between Clifton and I, because in my house, divorce was NOT an option. This is my testimony!

While fighting for my marriage, I learned that I could not depend on my feelings (heart) to guide my decisions. In the past, "depending on my feelings" played a colossal role in undermining my marriage. *The Bible says:*

The heart is deceitful above all things, and desperately wicked: who can know it? (Jeremiah 17:9 [KJV])

> *He that trusteth in his own heart is a fool: but whoso walketh wisely, shall be delivered. (Proverbs 28:26 [KJV])*

Unfortunately, "depending on my feelings" caused me to say negative things about my marriage - because I felt my anger was justified. Honestly, I did not truly understand the power of my words until I really began to understand these scriptures:

> *But the tongue can no man tame; it is an unruly evil, full of deadly poison. (James 3:8 [KJV])*

> *Death and life are in the power of the tongue: and they that love it shall eat the fruit thereof. (Proverbs 18:21 [KJV])*

> *The tongue of the wise useth knowledge aright: but the mouth of fools poureth out foolishness. (Proverbs 15:2 [KJV])*

> *The words of a wise man's mouth are gracious and win him favor, but the lips of*

> *a fool consume him. (Ecclesiastes 10:12 [AMP])*

I also did not know who I was in Christ. In other words, I did not, at the time, understand that as a Child of God, I am a joint-heir with Christ, sharing His inheritance with Him (Romans 8:17). I also did not know that I have direct access to God (Ephesians 2:18). Likewise, I did not know that God works through me to help me do the things he wants me to do (Philippians 2:13). Most importantly, I did not know that I am complete in Jesus Christ, and strengthened by his glorious power (Colossians 1:11).

> *And since we are his children, we are his heirs. In fact, together with Christ we are heirs of God's glory. But if we are to share his glory, we must also share his suffering. (Romans 8:17 [NLT])*

> *Now all of us can come to the Father through the same Holy Spirit because of*

what Christ has done for us. (Ephesians 2:18 [NLT])

For God is working in you, giving you the desire and the power to do what pleases him. (Philippians 2:13 [NLT])

We also pray that you will be strengthened with all his glorious power so you will have all the endurance and patience you need. May you be filled with joy. (Colossians 1:11 [NLT])

The Wedding Day

Your wedding day has come. The place is filled with decorations, family, and friends - all there for you and your groom. But, it dawns on you that you are getting married for show – not love, but it's too late to turn back. So, you go through with the wedding. You stand before God and all of your loved ones, and say vows to your soon-to-be spouse that you are not prepared to fulfill. As the day goes on, you put on a fake smile for the videos, cameras, family, and friends. You even dance a little with your new spouse. But, all the while you're thinking, "Did I just make the biggest mistake of my life?" The thought is unbearable, so you pretend to be happy. Try as you might to hold it all in, when your family and friends congratulate you, you begin to weep. Sadly, your loved ones think you are crying because you are so overwhelmed with love and joy, but in reality, you are crying because you know you are not ready for marriage.

That was once me – partly. Oftentimes, people get married for the wrong reasons, then, they either wind up in a healthy marriage or a troubled union that is on the verge of divorce. Well, originally my husband and I got married at a local courthouse, then a couple of months later, we had an *actual* wedding - you know, with fancy decorations, clothes, food, and way too many guests. Yes, our wedding was very glamorous and elegant. We wanted it that way. You see, when we initially got married at the courthouse, we had only been together for nine months. I had just ended a long-term relationship, and Clifton had recently divorced.

And, as you probably guessed, I became pregnant during the first three months of our relationship. So, I agreed to marry Clifton because I was pregnant and only because I was pregnant. Truthfully, I did not want to bring a child into this world without being married. "Cliché," you say, to which I respond, "Absolutely not." The Bible teaches us that fornication is a sin, and we are to control our bodies.

> *God's will is for you to be holy, so stay away from all sexual sin. Then each of you will control his own body[a] and live in holiness and honor—not in lustful passion like the pagans who do not know God and his ways. (I Thessalonians 4:3–5 [NLT])*

I wanted to make things *right*, so I got married without thinking twice. On the day we got married at the courthouse, I was almost eight months pregnant. I looked my groom in his eyes – and lied. I did not *really* "love" him. And, I was not ready for marriage; yet, I still felt that I had to prove something to God…and everyone else. Prove something to God, now that's funny, but that was my perspective, at the time.

Of course, Clifton and I did have history - we went to the same high school, went on one or two dates, hung out together, and shared the same friends. I knew his family, and he knew mine. We were, however, "in love" with the teens we remembered each other to be, but we were not "in love" with the adults we had become. But, that type of love is NOT enough! Our foundation was weak—we did not know each other—but we got married anyways.

After getting married at the courthouse, I reaped all of the benefits of being a military spouse, although, I did not claim my husband, as my spouse until eight months later - on our "wedding day." I also did not change my last name, and we did not move in together until about two months after we got married. We did not even communicate all that well, and we were not intimate.

Before our wedding, things had been getting worse by the day, but deep down I hoped it was simply due to the added stress of planning a wedding, having our first child, and going back to school. In other words, I convinced myself that things would get better after the wedding, and that my feelings were simply *nothing*. And, honestly, on our wedding day, I felt a sense of relief. I really did enjoyed being with him.

During our wedding, as we stood before God, family, and friends, I felt a little different. I thought, "This is it. I love this guy, and maybe, I did not make a mistake, after all." Truthfully, I had been asking, "Is this the right guy for me?" for a while. I did not realize it at the time, but I should have been asking myself, "Am I developing into the right person?" The truth is there is no real way of knowing, if you married the right person. For example, you could very well marry the right person, but treat that "right" person wrong. Thus, when issues arise and divorce or separation lurks on the horizon, you could still find yourself asking, "Is he or she the right person for me?" especially, if you are not developing into the individual God wants you to be.

Fake It Till You Make It or NOT

After the wedding, and our family and friends had left, reality began to set in, and we were left with only each other and our son. That was when the real work began. Unfortunately, after about a year of marriage, we still had not grown as a couple. In fact, we were steadily growing apart. Our relationship had taken a turn for the worse, even though we appeared to be a happily married couple to others. Right before my eyes, my marriage was falling apart, and I did not have—nor, did I want the courage or strength to fight for my marriage. My husband was a Marine, so he was always working or away from home. But, when he was home, his insecurities caused us to argue more than anything. We also did not go on many family outings, because our finances were always an issue, which stemmed from poor communication. I was angry most of the time, and our relationship lacked intimacy. I did not respect him, nor, did I receive any affection from him. As a result, I began to develop a mind-set of a single mom, who was only married on paper.

The single-mom mentality stemmed partly from our poor communication and intimacy, and my husband's long work hours (i.e. multiple trainings and deployments). I also felt that my husband spent little time with our son, even though he said he was doing the best that he could. Most of our conversations centered on money and parenting—nothing more and nothing less. I did not trust my husband to make decisions about our son, because he was barely there. Moreover, my concept of marriage and parenting was distorted, because I never got to see what marriage *should* look like, or have a father figure to show me what a father is *supposed* to do.

My mom was a single mother of four. She struggled to make ends meet, became a victim of domestic violence, and still managed to make sure me and my siblings had everything we needed growing up. As a result, I went with what was familiar to me. In other words, I did what I saw my mom do. I took care of our son, regardless of what was happening to me personally. I made *everything* about our son, and as a result, I ended up neglecting my marriage.

I dismissed my husband's presence, focusing on me and my son. I became an expert at ignoring Clifton, who I put down and humiliated every chance I got. Truthfully, my husband was and still is a great provider - he has always made sure we had *everything* we needed, despite my actions.

However, I wanted Clifton to be an active participant in raising our son, but I did not know how to tell him that – in a way that he could understand. I wanted my husband to watch our son a few hours, give him a bath, make sure he had his medications, and do more chores, without having to ask him to do those things. But, I never communicated my desires to him in his "language," because I did not know how.

I believed that my anger and withdrawal from him and our relationship would help him recognize the issues and fix them, but that was an unrealistic expectation on my part. *How does someone fix something when he or she doesn't know a problem even exists?* Impossible. So, as I was humiliating my husband, and not being submissive, my actions prevented him from *wanting to be around*, and unfortunately, my son suffered from my actions. My distorted thinking about marriage and parenting crippled my decision-making skills, which kept me from overcoming my challenges.

In fact, one day after work, my husband came home, and said, "One of my Marines invited us to church, would you like to go?" I ignored him, so he asked again.

With an attitude I said, "Sure…I do not have any place else to go." I was trying to tell him we did not spend enough time together, and we really did not know each other without verbally saying the words. *We needed to fix it.* Obviously, he could not read my mind, but I still believed my needs were apparent from the tone of my voice.

So, as I sat in church that Sunday, it dawned on me how much pain I was really in – more than I was willing to admit to my husband. I was very angry about my marital problems! Nevertheless, my husband and I kept going to church, and together we attached ourselves to New Beginnings Ministry of Faith under the leadership of Bishop Charles and Pastor Marion Dudley. Attaching ourselves to this ministry was the beginning of turning our marriage around. However, it did not happen instantly.

At first, I was not willing to hear God's Word, and allow it to be planted in me, so I could grow, and allow God's plan for marriage to manifest in my own marriage. More specifically, I had to renew my mind (Romans 12:2) with regard to what the Bible says about marriage and love, casting away my transgressions (Ezekiel 18:31), having faith, doing the work, and embracing God's plan. When your mind is not renewed, you are left depending only on your own understanding (Proverbs 3:5–6). The Bible teaches us that faith without works is dead (James 2:26), and that our actions allow our faith to be complete. In fact, even Abraham's actions had to line up with his faith, as he offered his son Isaac on the altar (James 2:21–22). *About all these matters, the Bible says*:

And be not conformed to this world: but be ye transformed by the renewing of your mind, that ye may prove what is that good, and acceptable, and perfect, will of God. (Romans 12:2 [KJV])

Cast away from you all your transgressions, whereby ye have transgressed; and make you a new heart and a new spirit. (Ezekiel 18:31 [KJV])

Trust in the Lord with all thine heart; and lean not unto thine own understanding. In all thy ways acknowledge him, and he shall direct thy paths. (Proverbs 3:5–6 [KJV])

> *Just as the body is dead without breath, so also faith is dead without good works. (James 2:26 [NLT])*

> *Don't you remember that our ancestor Abraham was shown to be right with God by his actions when he offered his son Isaac on the altar? You see, his faith and his actions worked together. His actions made his faith complete. (James 2:21–22 [NLT])*

It is no secret that many people have false preconceived notions about marriage, and what it takes to have a happy, healthy marital union. Bishop Dudley once said, "The person you marry is not the person you dated." At first, I could not comprehend the meaning of this statement, but by the end of his message, I had a big "aha" moment. It dawned on me that his statement implied that when you date someone, you put on your best shoes (behavior) to appease him or her. However, in reality, your best shoes in the dating world is not the *real* you. *Why not?* Well, because we are human, which means we are all flawed.

Think about it - you probably did not communicate everything that bothered you, while you were dating, because you tolerated those things. *Why?* Because, you loved that person, and were willing to do anything for him or her. However, once you married, the very things you tolerated before became intolerable in your marriage. Therefore, the more you learn about your spouse, the more you learn how to better communicate and be more vocal about the things that bother you.

As a result, you and/or your spouse can freely say to one another, "I did not know that bothered you..." That is why it is so important to understand that love is transitional. In other words, it has to be learned. As you and your spouse grow and change so does your love. But, you have to be willing to view love as a sacrifice. More specifically, it is important to sacrifice your wants and desires for your spouse's. When you do this, it allows love to become a choice. So, when this lesson was revealed to me, I knew that I needed improvement in this area.

As months went by, we became actively involved in the church. We began attending Sunday and midweek services regularly, going to church fellowships, volunteering most of our time at church, and surrounding ourselves with couples, who had healthy marriages. Yet, we still refused to face the demons in our marriage. We were frauds, and we both knew it. And, honestly, I grew envious of the allegedly *perfect* relationships around me. So, in front of our church family, we pretended to be happy, but behind closed doors, we were heartbroken, angry, and ready to walk out on each other. In fact, we had become so distant from each other and our problems that we literally did not know how to communicate with each other - if we did not have other people around. I felt extremely awkward being with my husband by myself.

As I was leaving church one day, I remember telling Pastor Dudley that I would not be coming in to volunteer the next day, because my husband and I had an appointment with a marriage counselor. I explained to her some of the issues we were facing, and she said, "When you guys have completed all of your counseling sessions, Bishop and I would love to help you better understand God's plan for marriage…so, if you want to talk, please let us know." Those few little words led to a life-changing relationship with Bishop and Pastor Dudley.

And, we did just that. After we completed our secular marriage counseling sessions, we started taking counsel under Bishop and Pastor Dudley, primarily because I could not shake my feelings of anger, bitterness, resentment, brokenness, loneliness, and emotional-detachment. But, as time went on, our marriage slowly started to change for the better. Bishop and Pastor Dudley began to put things into perspective, according to what the Bible says.

One of the first concepts my husband and I learned can be found in Genesis 2:24, "Therefore shall a man leave his father and his mother, and shall cleave unto his wife: and they shall be one flesh" (KJV). We had already begun to shift our loyalties towards each other (leaving), but it was still too difficult to build a continual relational bond (cleaving), as we were emotionally detached from each other. So, we were urged to use the tool we were given - the Bible.

We were instructed to use the Bible, as a manual to guide our decision making skills in our marriage. Bishop and Pastor Dudley showed us with Ephesians 5:23 and 5:25–26 how I was supposed to allow my husband to love and lead me. *I was not doing that.* In fact, every chance I got, I pushed him away, and intentionally disagreed with him. For instance, if he said the car was dark blue; I said it was black. I built walls to guard my heart, and I would not tear them down for us to become emotionally-attached.

In order for my husband to love and lead me, we learned that he had to nourish, cherish, and pay attention to me (Ephesians 5:28–29). In other words, Clifton had to learn and do little things to make me smile, learn my likes and dislikes, say kind words to uplift me, show affection towards me, and take care of not only my needs but some of my wants as well. Unfortunately, I did not feel he was doing that. The following words did not ring true at the time:

> *For the husband is head of the wife, as Christ is head of the church, Himself being the Savior of the body. (Ephesians 5:23 [AMP])*

> *For husbands, this means love your wives, just as Christ loved the church. He gave up his life for her to make her holy and clean, washed by the cleansing of God's word. (Ephesians 5:25–26 [NLT])*

> *So ought men to love their wives as their own bodies. He that loveth his wife loveth himself. For no man ever yet hated his own flesh; but nourisheth and cherisheth it, even as the Lord the church. (Ephesians 5:28–29 [KJV])*

The importance of submission, love and respect, and support backed by biblical principles—found in Ephesians 5:21–24, Colossians 3:18, and Proverbs 31:10–12—were also made clear under the counsel of Bishop and Pastor Dudley, as these are the roles of husbands and wives. Through them, I learned that submission is not about controlling your spouse, but loving and respecting your spouse just as you would Christ.

It is my responsibility to be my husband's helper. I am supposed to encourage my husband and cheer him on. And, my attitude and actions are supposed to coincide with what my mouth is saying, and most importantly, I am supposed to follow my husband's leadership. He, on the other hand, is supposed to submit to how I desired to be love. In other words, it is his responsibility to love me beyond my flaws and recognize his desires, while meeting mine.

Submitting yourselves one to another in the fear of God. Wives, submit yourselves unto your own husbands, as unto the Lord. For the husband is the head of the wife, even as Christ is the head of the church: and he is the saviour of the body. Therefore as the church is subject unto Christ, so let the

> *wives be to their own husbands in every thing. (Ephesians 5:21–24 [KJV])*

> *Wives, submit yourselves unto your own husbands, as it is fit in the Lord. (Colossians 3:18 [KJV])*

> *Who can find a virtuous and capable wife? She is more precious than rubies. Her husband can trust her, and she will greatly enrich his life. She brings him good, not harm, all the days of her life. (Proverbs 31:10–12 [NLT])*

At first, I needed to constantly remind myself that God wanted me to be submissive, which meant training my tongue to speak life (Isaiah 55:11) into our marriage, but I was not doing that. This task proved to be very difficult for me. I was not being completely transparent with my husband about the hurt and pain I held inside. I needed to communicate this to him if I wanted to heal. I was foolish—"The wise woman builds her house, but with her own hands the foolish one tears hers down" (Proverbs 14:1 [NIV]).

I allowed the enemy to use me to tear down my own marriage, because I had lost my identity. In the process of trying to understand marriage, be a good parent, obtain my master's degree, and seek employment, I had become a stranger to myself. I did not know my own likes and dislikes, because I had buried them. As a result, we found ourselves in a vicious cycle.

Our marriage would be great for a while, and then we would revert back to our old habits, which caused trouble for us. The lack of communication and issues regarding our finances resurfaced. I started ignoring him again—feeling angry, frustrated, and alone—and not being intimate. He started being controlling, distant, and withholding money. This went on for three additional years. We masked the fact that we were unhappy. My husband began to work longer hours, and I overloaded myself with schoolwork by starting my doctoral program. I also started a new job and tried to spend as much time, as humanly possible at church. My goal was to avoid addressing our marital issues.

Well, after four years of marriage, while still pretending to be happily married in public, but broken behind closed doors, we were on the verge of calling it quits. By this time though, we were in a totally different place of brokenness. We knew what the Bible said about marriage, but we were just too selfish to change our behaviors, and implement the Word. When you know what to do, but choose not to do it, you are in sin, according to James 4:17. We were living in sin, but trying to cover it up and prosper at the same time. We ignored the Bible's proclamation: "whoever conceals their sins does not prosper, but the one who confesses and renounces them finds mercy." (Proverbs 28:13 [NIV]).

It seemed like we had already accepted defeat. We were not going beyond our emotions, and giving our maximum effort to step into what God had already pre-destined for our marriage. You see, when God has a plan for your life or has called you to do something, you must put forth maximum effort, and live by faith (Hebrews 10:38).

Honestly, I am not proud of my actions, and I'll be the first to admit that, at some point, I turned from the Word towards the world. In other words, I thought God was not working fast enough, because I was unable to see His promises manifest in my marriage the way I thought they should. I dismissed the Bible's teaching that we should be anxious for nothing (Philippians 4:6–7). I always knew that the world did not hold the answers to fixing my troubled marriage, because the answers I sought were housed in the Word. But, I refused to accept this because I did not want to wait any longer. *I was wrong.*

I had the tools to make my marriage better, yet, I stubbornly refused to put forth the effort needed to build a happy, healthy marriage. So, ultimately, my inaction caused my marriage to suffer. I now know that putting God's plan on the backburner only highlighted my foolishness and disobedience. As a result, I was disqualified from receiving the unlimited blessings of God through my marriage. You see, the Bible tells us that if we put God first, all blessings will be available to us (Matthew 6:33).

Therefore to him that knoweth to do good, and doeth it not, to him it is sin. (James 4:17 [KJV])

Do not be anxious about anything, but in every situation, by prayer and petition, with thanksgiving, present your requests to God. And the peace of God, which transcends all understanding, will guard your hearts and your minds in Christ Jesus. (Philippians 4:6–7 [NIV])

So will My word be which goes out of My mouth; It will not return to Me void (useless, without result), Without accomplishing what I desire, And without succeeding in the matter for which I sent it. (Isaiah 55:11 [AMP])

And my righteous ones will live by faith. But I will take no pleasure in anyone who turns away. (Hebrews 10:38 [NLT])

But seek ye first the kingdom of God, and his righteousness; and all these things shall be added unto you. (Matthew 6:33 [KJV])

Enough Is Enough

As I continued to volunteer at church and struggle with my troubled marriage, I slowly fell into depression. In the process of pretending to be something I was not, I lost myself and my happiness. I did not love myself, let alone my spouse. I had lied about the condition of my marriage for so long that I fell out of touch from reality. The more I faked being happily married, the more constricted I became. I was in a jail of my own making.

And, I hated who I had become. My negative thoughts only pushed me deeper and deeper into bondage. I honestly believe that the enemy had control over my thoughts, when it came to my marriage, those negative thoughts were affecting every area of my life. Until I learned how to receive God's unconditional love, I exempted myself from the promises of God.

Bishop and Pastor Dudley sensed that something was not quite right; yet, they never pressured me to talk about it. They did, however, repeatedly let me know that their door was always open. Nevertheless, I pushed through, until one Sunday. While Bishop Dudley taught about choices, I had an epiphany. That was when I said to myself, "Enough is enough!" During that sermon, Bishop, taught me that we all face life-choice moments, which are "moments in time, when you are faced with difficult situations." The choice, during these moments, must be made in faith—trusting God for a favorable outcome to difficult situations.

During these moments, when you are tasked with making a decision, the goal is to *expect* God to provide a supernatural move that will affect your present circumstances. Ironically, after all of the years I spent in church, it was Bishop's sermon on choices that was my *moment* with God. *I had finally gotten it.* I finally understood what God had been trying to tell me. I was responding to my troubled marriage in fear, frustration, and fraudulence (by pretending to be happy).

I had to learn how my decision-making process towards my marriage was vital for the success of my marriage. It was during this time, that I truly began to understand that God would not present me with a dire situation without a steady life boat. If I was going to allow God to break my stronghold, I had to learn how to analyze my decisions, confess my misdeeds according to the Will of God, and wait patiently for Him to respond. To facilitate this process, I began doing things differently. I could not expect different results, if I continued to do the same things. *That would be insane!* My beliefs slowly changed, and my beliefs became a direct reflection of how I saw myself and my decisions.

So, instead of being envious, I started to "copy" the things I saw other healthy married couples do in their own marriages. In fact, one married couple really stood out to me, the Ponders. When I first met them, I did not know their history, nor was I aware of any challenges they had faced, but what I did know was that every time I saw them, they were always smiling and being affectionate towards each other.

I remember thinking, "Now, that is a couple my husband and I need to get to know better." As we started hanging out more and more with the Ponders, and I started exercising with Mrs. Ponder, I began to think more and more about this confession: "God is raising up somebody, somewhere, to use their power and their ability to help me." You see, I had been saying this confession and holding it close to my heart since I began attending New Beginnings Ministry of Faith, and I now was actually starting to believe it. In other words, I was beginning to see it manifest in my life and my marriage.

And, amazingly, the Ponders were truly genuine in their affection towards each other. Mrs.

Ponder always greeted her husband when he came home, and her face always lit up every time she saw him. She placed her wants and needs aside to address her husband's, and together they managed to laugh even when they disagreed. Mrs. Ponder and I connected, having conversations that eventually lead to her giving me marital advice. Moreover, she always—and yes, I do mean *always*—backed up advice with scripture passages. At times, I thought, "She is doing a bit too much," but, honestly, it was what I needed. God placing the right people in my life, so they could show me how believers are *supposed* to walk. *Finally, I had a glimpse of what a successful marriage looked like.*

    In addition, the more time I spent with Bishop and Pastor Dudley, the more I emulated Pastor Dudley. I watched how she spoke to Bishop in such a kind way, encouraging him, fixing his plate (during fellowship dinners), laughing at the jokes (even when she didn't find them funny), bringing him lunch (just because), and so much more. *So, I started doing that for my husband.* I spoke nice words to my husband (even when I wanted to speak negatively). Most of all, I *stopped* tearing him down and *started* telling him how much I truly appreciated him.

I also made sure he had dinner every night and I affirmed that he was not my enemy. His feelings mattered just as much as my own. In other words, I started to respect him. After I started doing this, my husband began saying, "I think you should hang around Pastor Dudley more often…you are acting different." My husband's statement led to the most positive conversation we had about our marriage in a long time. In fact, by the end of it, I felt a sense of accomplishment.

I thanked God at that very moment for allowing me to not get weary, while doing good and giving me the strength to continue, even when it seemed like my husband was not recognizing my efforts, as I waited for God to bring about a shift in our relationship (Galatians 6:9, Isaiah 40:31). I made the commitment to walk by faith (2 Corinthians 5:7) and allow God to heal me and my marriage this time (for real, for real). I was desperate, and this desperate time called for desperate prayers and actions. So, I worked every day to rid myself from my bad habits – a catalyst for much of the issues in my troubled marriage.

Let us not become weary in doing good, for at the proper time we will reap a harvest if we do not give up. (Galatians 6:9 [NIV])

But they that wait upon the Lord shall renew their strength; they shall mount up with wings as eagles; they shall run, and not be weary; and they shall walk, and not faint. (Isaiah 40:31 [KJV])

For we walk by faith, not by sight. (2 Corinthians 5:7 [KJV])

Therefore if any man be in Christ, he is a new creature: old things are passed away; behold, all things are become new. (2 Corinthians 5:17 [KJV])

My husband was right. I was behaving differently. I wanted to change for me. I wanted to be happy and love myself again, so I began to change my perspective.

I made myself fully available to God (Roman 12:1–10), so God could heal my brokenness. I learned that I was the reason my marriage was in trouble for so long. It was my choice. I also accepted the truth - I did not love my husband, which led me to be angry, depressed, mean, and unsupportive of him. I did not communicate properly, and I withheld intimacy. You see, God never promised us a life free of trials and tribulations that would never test our faith.

Rather, He promised us that "no weapon that is formed against thee shall prosper, and every tongue that shall rise against thee in judgment thou shalt condemn" (Isaiah 54:17 [KJV]). I was ignorant, I know that now. And, in the process of turning from the Word towards the world, I lost my focus on God's plan for my marriage, and negated that His plan for my marriage is to prosper (Jeremiah 29:11). As a result, I became vulnerable to the enemy's attacks.

For I know the thoughts that I think toward you, saith the Lord, thoughts of peace, and not of evil, to give you an expected end. (Jeremiah 29:11 [KJV])

As I began to change my attitude, and the way I interacted with my husband, he began to do the same. He began to recognize my desire to change, and became less controlling. I no longer felt that we had this strange father-daughter–like relationship. He began to encourage me and give me compliments, and we began to communicate a little more. We started making decisions that would enhance the growth of our marriage. We started going to marriage conferences and marriage retreats. We were learning how to cope with our anger, effectively communicate, seek forgiveness, grant forgiveness, and, most importantly, apply scriptures to our marriage.

Even though our relationship was getting better, and we were working hard to improve it, something was still missing. My husband had transformed right before my eyes. And, truthfully, he was growing and changing faster than me. He was also becoming a man, whose faith had increased. A man, who was applying the Bible's principles to his life. A man, who understood the concept of loving and leading his wife. And, a man, who wholeheartedly stood in reverence of God. *I, however, was stuck.* My progress had slowed almost to a halt, because I was still broken inside. I thought I could move forward without addressing problems from the past, but I was wrong.

Clifton wanted to get to the root our problems and fix them, according to the Word, but I kept saying, "Let it go…I'm over it…I'm good." I truly believed that if I pretended the problems did not exist, they would go away, and I could move forward with my life. But, eventually, I realized that could not happen (Jeremiah 6:14). *Why not?* I was still harboring hurt in my heart, which prevented me from spiritually growing and healing. This hurt was also preventing me from experiencing the blessings of God. This trying time reminded me of Psalms 30:2 and Psalms 147:3. It was only through God and me walking in my truth that my brokenness would be healed.

I needed to communicate my issues to Clifton because they were damaging our marriage. I also needed to find the courage to confront all our issues, one at a time. Likewise, I needed to forgive him, as Christ forgave me (Ephesians 4:32; Matthew 6:14–15), so I could begin to work diligently with him to repair and rebuild our relationship. Thus, I began the journey of confronting my hurt by communicating my truth.

My people are broken—shattered!—and they put on Band-Aids, saying, "It's not so bad. You'll be just fine." But, things are not "just fine!" (Jeremiah 6:14 [The Message])

O LORD, my God, I cried unto thee, and thou hast healed me. (Psalms 30:2 [KJV])

He healeth the broken in heart, and bindeth up their wounds. (Psalms 147:3 [KJV])

And be ye kind one to another, tenderhearted, forgiving one another, even as God for Christ's sake hath forgiven you. (Ephesians 4:32 [KJV])

For if ye forgive men their trespasses, your heavenly Father will also forgive you: But if ye forgive not men their trespasses, neither will your Father forgive your trespasses. (Matthew 6:14–15 [KJV])

The Truth Heals

Vocalizing my truth to my husband was one of the most challenging, yet essential things I have ever done, in regards to my marriage. No, it was not because I had a problem telling the truth or because I am a habitual liar; it was because I was afraid. I was afraid of hurting his feelings, and reverting back to how things were. I did not want to go back to not communicating, not being supportive and submissive, not being intimate, and not doing everything else we were doing to "fix" in our marriage.

With the help of God, we had made so much progress, and I did not want to jeopardize that. Isaiah 41:10 states that I cannot allow my fear to prevent me from going to the next level in my marriage. After all, the Bible tells us, "For God hath not given us the spirit of fear; but of power and of love, and of a sound mind" (2 Timothy 1:7 [KJV]). Therefore, I had to speak my truth in order for us to address our issues, one at a time.

In other words, I could no longer allow my thoughts to shape my beliefs and prevent me from experiencing God's plan. So, my husband and I began to have several conversations about our marriage (how and why our marriage was trouble). As we were having these conversations, I wept. I was finally releasing the hurt and pain I held inside. It felt as though a heavy burden had been lifted off my shoulders. I no longer had to pretend with him, and I could be honest about my issues. *I was no longer caring that extra baggage of brokenness.*

Don't be afraid, for I am with you. Don't be discouraged, for I am your God. I will

> *strengthen you and help you. I will hold you up with my victorious right hand. (Isaiah 41:10 [NLT])*

As we entered year six of our marriage, I began to communicate to Clifton the truth about my issues. Not loving my husband was one of the major truths that I confessed to him. It was also the foundation of all of our issues. My husband never knew I did not love him until I told him. He knew I was unhappy, and he thought my actions were the result of my unhappiness. But, the reality was that my actions were a result of not loving him. I remember, while having this conversation, feeling extremely vulnerable. As I sat on the couch, right beside him, the conversation about happiness unfolded. We talked about what we both could do to improve our marriage. When it was my turn to respond, I remember repeating, "I don't know, I don't know, I don't know."

Afterwards, he asked me, "So, you can't think of anything you can do to improve our marriage?"

Tears started cascading down my cheeks, and I knew at that moment I needed to tell the truth. I replied, "I do not want to hurt your feelings - just don't worry about it. I will figure it out." But, Clifton did not give up, and I thank God for that.

As I shared with my husband that I never allowed myself to love him, as my spouse, he started to cry. Despite the tears, I pushed on and told him that I loved the person he had become. I explained to him that for a long time I did not love myself, because I had not released past hurts from previous relationships. I had to do that before I could love myself, and in turn love him. I expressed to him that I recognized we were in a better place in our marriage, but I was not overcoming my past hurts, as quickly as him. I also talked to him about the battle within myself, due to the lack of love I had for myself.

I needed for him to understand that it was not his fault, he was not the reason I did not love him. I simply had not allowed myself to love him. No, my husband did not respond in anger or try to retaliate; rather, he forgave me just as Ephesian 4:32 commands.

Once I shared with Clifton what I should have revealed years ago, he explained some of his mistakes, spoke on some of the things he did wrong over the years, and apologized. He also admitted that he still had much to learn about how to love and lead me. And, my husband made the choice to give me time to learn how to love him. In other words, he *chose* to accept me just as I was. He *chose* to love me. Clifton decided to love me, just as Christ loved the church.

And, be ye kind to one to another, tenderhearted, forgiving one another, even as God for Christ's sake hath forgiven you. (Ephesians 4:32 [KJV])

After our conversation on not being in love, the conversations that followed were not as difficult, but still very necessary. We continued addressing each issue one at a time, and we discussed the concept of control versus submission in-depth. I remember sitting on the edge of the bed, as my husband was getting dressed. I watched him in silence. And, as he was about to walk out of the room, I said to him, "You were controlling in the past, you know that right?" He stopped, and looked at me, then, walked over to the edge of our bed, and sat down.

He replied, "Why didn't you say something then?" Without answering his question, I continued talking. I explained to him that it was his controlling behavior that partly caused my withdrawal from him. I also explained that in the past, he used money to control me. And, without allowing him to speak, I proceeded to tell him that any time he wanted me to do something, not to do something, or view things his way, he used money, as a bargaining chip. I wanted him to know that because of his behavior, I chose not to respect him or consider his wants and needs. I further explained that, during that time, it felt like he was treating me like a child, which prevented me from *wanting* to be intimate with him.

As he sat there, listening to my truth, he validated my feelings. He said, "Meka, you are so right, and I'm truly sorry." There was no blame-shifting or back-and-forth between, as we continued our conversation. He simply explained to me that he did not intentionally do those things. More specifically, it was never his intention to control me or make me feel like we had a father-daughter relationship. *He just wanted to be a great provider.* He said, "Truthfully, I was not being the husband that God wanted me to be for you back then." He went on to say that he carried issues from his first marriage into our marriage.

Of course, as we sat and discussed how unhealthy it was to bring issues from our previous relationships into our marriage, closure was brought to the issue. From that moment on, decision making between us became a lot easier because we started listening to each other more and learned how to better validate each other's feelings. Clifton also made sure that I always had something (money) in my pocket. And, as a result, I began to respect him as my husband and so much more. I respected his honesty, and his ability to recognize his mistakes and apologize for them.

A couple of months later, we had the intimacy conversation. We needed to address several issues in this area. First we addressed past issues that were affecting how we interacted with each other. Then, we shared our expectations and desires with one another. You see, when my husband and I were in a really bad place in our marriage, intimacy and romance were not present and had not been present for little over a year.

There was no commitment, companionship, passion, or even spiritual intimacy between us. We had not been communicating, spending time together or displaying our love for each other through any type non-sexual affection. We did not have a healthy attitude towards one another, and we didn't really respect each other. Most importantly, we were not connecting spiritually, because we were not praying and reading the Word regularly, as a couple.

I tried to help my husband understand that we lacked true intimacy, because I did not allow myself to reveal to him areas of my life that were not readily available to others. In other words, I was not allowing him to get to know me. Truthfully, I did not even know myself. I also explained to my husband that my lack of sexual desire was a symptom of other issues (i.e. communication, finances, parenting, affection, anger, bitterness, resentment, frustration, and hopelessness) in our marriage.

In other words, the brokenness and hurt I felt seemed too difficult to overcome, so that I could allow myself to experience true intimacy. Clifton listened then explained that a man's sexuality is primarily expressed through sexual intercourse. According to my husband, as I was emotionally disconnecting myself from our marriage, I was denying him the ability to feel desired (1 Corinthians 7:3–5), which was not right. He then proceeded to let me know that the more I became emotionally disconnected and withdrawn from intimacy and romance, the more he was tempted to step outside our marriage. Thankfully, he never did.

> *The husband should fulfill his wife's sexual needs, and the wife should fulfill her husband's needs. The wife gives authority over her body to her husband, and the husband gives authority over his body to his wife. Do not deprive each other of sexual relations, unless you both agree to*

> *refrain from sexual intimacy for a limited time so you can give yourselves more completely to prayer. Afterward, you should come together again so that Satan won't be able to tempt you because of your lack of self-control. (1 Corinthians 7:3–5 [NLT])*

When we became fully aware of what the lack of intimacy and romance did to our marriage, I began to thank God, and ask for forgiveness. God intended for us to explore marital intimacy and romance to celebrate oneness before Him by communicating with each other, spending time together, showing our love through sexual and non-sexual affection, and praying and reading the Word together, as a couple.

During this time, I informed my husband that I would make sex a priority in our marriage, and as a result, he felt much better about our relationship. However, for me to fulfill that promise, I had to make sure he understood that sex for me was linked to affection. I explained that it is difficult for me to be affectionate with him, if I am angry, frustrated, disappointed, tired, hurt, or overworked, or if I feel that my wants and needs are not important. He then made it clear to me that sex for him is a need, and if his sexual desires are fulfilled, there is a greater chance that the other issues will also be resolved. And, just like that the problem solved. I thought to myself, "We should have had this conversation a long time ago." Nevertheless, I still had to remind myself of 1 Corinthians 7:3–5. The more we talked and addressed our issues, the more I began to open my heart to loving my husband. God was healing my brokenness. He was showing me that my healing was in my truth. I could no longer ignore my truth, and expect the blessings of God to manifest within me and my marriage.

The Bible says, "the LORD is close to the brokenhearted; he rescues those whose spirits are crushed" (Psalms 34:18 [NLT]). As I became more honest with myself and my husband, and confessed the things I was too afraid to talk about, I was able to break free of my own sinful desire (John 8:32; James 5:16). I was finally healing from my past hurt. The act of speaking my truth was a catalyst for my healing. Confessing my truth and breaking my silence about the issues that plagued my marriage, were a part of God's plan for my healing. So, I ask you, what is your truth(s) that's holding you in bondage and preventing you from rebuilding your marriage?

> *And, ye shall know the truth, and the truth shall set you free. (John 8:32 [KJV])*

> *Confess your sins to each other and pray for each other so you may be healed. The earnest prayer of the righteous person has great power and produces wonderful results. (James 5:16 [NLT])*

Loving Your Spouse

You may have heard some people say, "You cannot help who you fall in love with." Not true! The fact is love is not only a feeling, but also a decision, one that involves sacrifice, selflessness, and transformation. Loving your spouse is not something that happens overnight. It takes a lot of effort from both parties. But, once you and your spouse say, "I do," you are not only connected to each other's aspirations and dreams, but also to each other's hurt, emotional baggage, flaws, worries, and doubts. *Therefore, you must remember that with love your marriage can withstand anything:*

Love is patient, love is kind. It does not envy, it does not boast, it is not proud. It does not dishonor others, it is not self-seeking, it is not easily angered, it keeps no record of wrongs. Love does not delight in evil but rejoices with the truth. It always protects, always trusts, always hopes, always perseveres. Love never fails. But where there are prophecies, they will cease; where there are tongues, they will be stilled; where there is knowledge, it will pass away. (1 Corinthians 13:4–8 [NIV])

Learning to love Clifton was essential to allowing God's plan for marriage to manifest in my own marriage. Once I allowed myself to be emotionally and spiritually healed by God, we were able to work through our issues and established boundaries for communication. I was also able to open my heart to love.

Embracing marriage, as a spiritual relationship, was significant to opening my heart to love. In fact, it was and still is, the foundation for learning how to love my husband unconditionally. You see, when two people are connected to God individually, and choose to walk with and obey God, through prayer and scripture; it opens the door to allow the power of God to work in their marriage. And, as a result, they are able to reflect the love of God and allow Christ to have total control over their lives.

Because, I so desperately wanted to reciprocate the love my husband showed me, when I did not love myself, it was essential for me to yield to the Holy Spirit. Yielding to the Holy Spirit meant that I had to get rid of the "I" perspective, and develop a "we" perspective.

Removing the "I" perspective involved removing my selfishness and pride, so I could cleave to my husband, and become one just as God tells us to in Genesis 2:18–24. Becoming one leads to a renewed commitment to submission, and submitting ourselves to each other is what scripture tells us to do (Ephesians 5:21).

Submitting to your spouse is hard to do, when you are not inspired. When I did not love Clifton, I had no inspiration to attempt to make our marriage work. In fact, we were both considering divorce. However, I chose to love Clifton, because I was inspired by the Word, and by the man he was becoming. I was also inspired by the blessing of God right before my eyes, manifesting in my marriage.

Furthermore, as I developed the "we" perspective, I began thinking, "What can *we* do to make our marriage better? How are *we* going to raise our child? How can *we* better communicate with each other? How are *we* going to address our finances? What can *we* do to increase intimacy and affection in our marriage? *We* are going to get through this despite what our situation currently looks like." So, once I allowed the Holy Spirit to guide me, while embracing the "we" perspective, my marriage began to reflect God's love.

Please understand that I did not choose to love my husband because our marriage was perfect and without disagreements; perfect it was not and still is not. In fact, yielding to the Holy Spirit, and choosing to love my husband did not prevent us from experiencing disagreements in our marriage. Remember, God never promised us a life free of discomfort and obstacles (Isaiah 54:17). As I grew in faith, however, and followed the principles recorded in scripture, I became better equipped to handle our disagreements. The truth is disagreements in marriages are common, and I believe they are meant to strengthen your marriage, if handled correctly. James 1:19–20 teaches us to be slow to speak and quick to listen. This is very important and is the foundation for handling disagreements correctly.

Understand this, my dear brothers and sisters: You must all be quick to listen, slow to speak, and slow to get angry. Human anger does not produce the righteousness God desires. (James 1:19–20 [NLT])

Here are a few tips that have helped me handle disagreements or conflicts in my marriage:

- ❖ Humble yourself before God, and ask Him to reveal what you contributed to the disagreement or conflict.
- ❖ Confess your anger to God before confronting your spouse.
- ❖ Ask God for forgiveness for your contribution to the disagreement or conflict.
- ❖ Thank God for His forgiveness. Be willing to seek forgiveness from your spouse, and grant forgiveness to your spouse.
- ❖ Allow each other to speak freely without shifting blame.
- ❖ Listen to each other, and strive to understand your spouse's perspective, instead of convincing your spouse to understand yours.
- ❖ Tell the truth.

- ❖ Do not leave a disagreement or conflict unresolved.
- ❖ Discuss one issue at a time.

Growing Your Love God's Way

Society teaches us that love is something that you fall in and out of, and it is supposed to be easy. Not so! Love is a choice that takes hard work, sacrifice, and patience. You and your spouse must learn to grow your love in God's way to have a successful marriage.

Choosing to love my spouse was a difficult task for me. Yes, I was attracted to my husband physically, but that did not mean I loved him. If anything, I was in lust with him—taken with his appearance and by how we bonded, when we first started dating. I really did not know how to love my husband.

Furthermore, I was battling with many issues from my past that had never been addressed, and those issues were slowly impacting my attitude, behavior, and beliefs. These issues became the fabric of my being, and my marriage reflected what I believed to be the truth at the time.

Before understanding God's plan for marriage, I had no idea of what my role as a wife should be. Therefore, I did what I saw other married couples do, while growing up: Fight and be selfish! So, the more I tried not to, the more I became like the very people I tried not to be. I did not know how to be a wife. I believed that I was entitled to be a mean person. I did not know how to properly address conflict that resulted in a win-win situation for me and my husband. I did not understand that by not loving myself, and knowing who I was, it would severely impact my marriage. *I did not know!*

Simply put, my thoughts molded my beliefs, and my beliefs impacted my actions, which led to poor choices in my marriage. It was only when I became honest with myself, taking the lies I had told myself over the years and replacing them with the truth of the Word of God that my thought process changed. I knew that breaking the cycle of dysfunctional marriages in my family had to start with me. So, with Jeremiah 29:11, Malachi 2:13–16, and Genesis 2:18–24, I reminded myself constantly that God has a plan for my marriage and my life. My mind was renewed, and my hurt and brokenness was healed (Romans 12:2; 2 Corinthians 10:5). I was no longer in the bondage of my past.

So, not just choosing to love, but also growing love is a choice. You must make a conscious effort every day to choose to grow your love with your spouse. Again, love is not a feeling or an attitude that can be turned on and off at any moment. The Bible helps us to understand this in 1 Corinthians 13. These verses discuss a love that withstands anything, despite the way we feel. Therefore, if you find yourself saying,

"I am not in love with my spouse anymore," that is not true. You have chosen not to love your spouse at that particular time. I know, this is probably a little difficult to comprehend.

For so long you may have been accustomed to associating love with your feelings and emotions, because that is what the world has taught you, but that is incorrect. Think of it this way - when there is trouble in your relationship, your love for your spouse becomes shaky, and you are ready to throw in the towel and give up, it is because the foundation that you have built your love upon is the world's system and not God's. In other words, you love your spouse, based on how the world says you should, and not how God desires you to do so. If you embrace God's principles on love and God's plan for marriage, you will not give up so quickly when you find yourself saying *"I'm not in love with him or her anymore."* You will also become better equipped to love your spouse God's way. Godly love reminds us that "love is patient, love is kind. It does not envy…It does not dishonor others, it is not self- seeking…It keeps no record of wrongs…It always protects, always trusts, always hopes, and always perseveres. Love never fails" (1 Corinthians 13:4–8 [NIV]).

Tips For Growing Your Love God's Way

While there is no one-size-fits-all plan for a successful marriage, please let the Word of God be your guide. It can be the navigational system for your marriage, as long as you choose to follow the directions. Taking a shortcut or deciding on what direction you will or will not follow will not result in God's plan for your marriage. But, once you grow your love God's way, you will not only better your relationship with your spouse, but also grow your relationship with God. *Here are a few tips to help you grow your love with your spouse, God's way:*

✓ **Tip 1: Make it Your Primary Goal in Your Marriage to Make Your Spouse Happy**

Be devoted to one another in love. Honor one another above yourselves. (Romans 12:10 [NIV])

When making your spouse happy becomes your primary goal in your marriage, by default you make a decision to put your spouse first. With all the "hustle and bustle" of everyday life, you may find yourself unintentionally neglecting your spouse, and putting others before him or her. Therefore, you must make a conscious effort to put your spouse first, spending quality time with him or her, and doing things that will make him or her happy. While you may spend a lot of time with your spouse doing everyday things, you should ask yourself, "How much of that time is truly quality time?"

Time designated just for you and your spouse becomes "us" time. Be it through date nights or mini-vacations, you must make time to focus on each other to grow your marriage. Do not allow the challenges of finances, children, or schedules prevent you from spending "us" time with your spouse. Be creative! Have fun! Laugh a little! Also, try to connect with your spouse during the day, while you are away from each other.

You can do this by sending each other short e-mails, video messages, text messages, and/or calling each other, during breaks. You can brighten your spouse's day and make him or her smile after a particularly rough day simply by sending him or her a message or calling him or her. When you do this, your time together when you reconnect at home becomes more meaningful. Little gestures like this will help to make your spouse happy.

✓ **Tip 2: Love and Respect Your Spouse**

Husbands, love your wives and do not be harsh with them. (Colossians 3:19 [NIV])

Better to live in a desert than with a quarrelsome and nagging wife. (Proverbs 21:19 [NIV])

Love is patient, love is kind. It does not envy, it does not boast, it is not proud. It does not dishonor others, it is not self-seeking, it is not easily angered, it keeps no record of wrongs. Love does not delight in evil but rejoices with the truth. It always

> *protects, always trusts, always hopes, and always perseveres. Love never fails… (1 Corinthians 13:4-8 [NIV])*

Do not get caught up in trying to change your spouse - just love him or her for who he or she is. Because, when you try to change your spouse, you are more prone to nagging, criticizing, disrespecting, and fault-finding.

No one is perfect, so expecting perfection from your spouse only leads to bitterness and resentment. Moreover, you cannot change your spouse, or make him or her conform to your wishes - only God can do that. You can, however, choose to love your spouse the way he or she is. So, spend less time trying to change your spouse, and more time trying to please him or her.

✓ Tip 3: Do Not be Afraid of Change and Court Your Spouse

My beloved spoke and said to me, "Arise my darling, my beautiful one, come with me." (Song of Solomon 2:10 [NIV])

It can be very easy for you to become complacent in your marriage and take your spouse for granted. However, you should not be afraid to try new things, and continue courting your spouse. When you and your spouse were dating, I'm sure you tried a few new activities together. *These activities made your relationship exciting, right?* Well, wine and dine your spouse in the same way you did when you were dating. This initiative will show your spouse that you are interested in him or her.

So, while sticking to what you know is OK, try new things that will ignite the spark in your relationship and improve the spontaneity in your marriage. I know, we have heard it all before - perhaps, you said it to your spouse or vice versa. *Does let's do something different, sound familiar?*

The truth is, marriages are successful when they are in line with God's plan for marriage. Therefore, love and happiness should be the foundation for your relationship, and you should strive to spend as much "us" time as possible, with your spouse to keep your love growing.

As you become more knowledgeable of God's plan for marriage, and you embrace that plan, your actions and perspective on being a spouse will change. So, be willing to recognize and change the very thing(s) you have always done and be prepared to alter your perspective on what it means to be a spouse, if it does not line up with the Word of God.

✓ **Tip 4: Appreciate Your Spouse**

Above all else, guard your heart, for everything you do flows from it. (Proverbs 4:23 [NIV])

As individuals, we are all flawed in some way. However, our flaws make up a part of who we are. In a marriage, it is easy to identify flaws in your spouse. For instance, you may not understand or dislike some of your spouse's habits, and before you know it, you are complaining. However, it is important to show gratitude. So, when you find yourself complaining about your spouse's flaws, think about the good things he or she does for you. In other words, appreciate your spouse for all he or she does.

Constantly having negative thoughts about your spouse, and repeatedly pointing out his or her flaws will eventually destroy your marriage. More specifically, the enemy will use your thoughts to trap you into believing the lies you tell yourself - lies like: "He or she does not appreciate me," "He or she does not understand me," "He or she does not listen to anything I say," and/or "He or she is so ungrateful."

Your thoughts influence the decisions you make, and those decisions guide your actions, which is why it is extremely important to show your spouse just how much you appreciate him or her. If you tell everyone around you how much you appreciate what your spouse does for you, but you never tell your spouse, then who benefits? No one!

✓ Tip 5: Invest in Your Marriage

As iron sharpens iron, so one person sharpens another. (Proverbs 27:17 [NIV])

Investing in your marriage will produce beneficial results for you and your spouse. You can invest in your marriage, by spending time at marriage retreats and conferences, and surrounding yourself with other married couples, who are looking to grow their marriages, according to the Word. Individuals who are committed to growing their marriage the way God intended are individuals of truth - not of facts. I've learned over the years that there is a difference between truth and facts.

It may be a fact that your spouse does not communicate well, and often makes decisions without you, or with little-to-no regard to how it will affect your family, but the truth is that the Word tells us to submit ourselves to one another. More specifically, individuals of truth speak the truth, which is the Word, because it helps your marriage become what God intended it to be.

So, in the same manner that you invest in business, education, or a career, you should invest in your marriage. That means that you have to sacrifice, put in work, and spend a little money—yes, purchase material aligned with the Word of God that will help you become a better spouse.

Do not neglect your marriage by not investing in it, because your results hinge on what you put into it. In other words, if you invest nothing, you get nothing. But, if you make a huge investment, you will reap a great harvest.

✓ Tip 6: Master the Art of Listening

A soft answer turneth away wrath: but grievous words stir up anger. (Proverbs 15:1 [KJV])

Wherefore, my beloved brethren, let every man be swift to hear, slow to speak, slow to wrath: For the wrath of man worketh not the righteousness of God. (James 1:19–20 [KJV])

Mastering the art of listening is an important part of effective communication. Often, we are too busy or too angry to really take the time to listen to our spouses. However, it is important to be in the moment to effectively communicate. More specifically, taking the time to listen to your spouse before responding allows for better communication.

When issues arise, it is your responsibility to confront your spouse, with the intention of listening. Don't let issues fester and linger, or these unresolved issues will turn into resentment and bitterness. Be willing to communicate your concerns with your spouse, even if you do not want to, or it seems difficult.

✓ **Tip 7: Resolve Conflict and Forget It**

Confess your faults one to another, and pray one for another, that ye may be healed. The effectual fervent prayer of a righteous man availeth much. (James 5:16 [KJV])

A person's wisdom yields patience; it is to one's glory to overlook an offense. (Proverbs 19:11 [NIV])

Be kind and compassionate to one another, forgiving each other, just as in Christ God forgave you. (Ephesians 4:32 [NIV])

"In your anger do not sin." Do not let the sun go down while you are still angry. (Ephesians 4:26 [NIV])

Communicating effectively and resolving conflicts go hand-in-hand. In other words, without being able to effectively communicate with your spouse, you cannot resolve conflicts. So, when an issue arises, ask yourself, "Is it worth it, or can I just let it go?" While some things are not worth fighting about, others should be addressed. Therefore, it is up to you and your spouse to determine what battles you will fight, and how you will handle them. The best course of action is to focus on one issue at a time, recognizing the part you played in the disagreement, being honest, trying to see things from your spouse's perspective, and being prepared to give and receive forgiveness.

Once the issue has been resolved, let it go! Do not come back two or three days later, and say, "Remember when you said [blah blah blah]... I did not like that, and I feel [blah blah blah]..." It's too late. In fact, it's almost like opening a jug of spoiled milk. It's worthless and may cause you and your spouse to enter into a cycle of unhealthy conflict resolution. Therefore, you must learn to let things go once you and your spouse have come to a resolution on an issue.

Also, do not go to bed angry. Small issues can quickly become bigger issues, after lingering in your mind for a while. If you need time to get your thoughts together, do so, but do not let your head hit the pillow, while still angry with your spouse. The Word tells us that "anger gives a foothold to the devil" (Ephesians 4:27 [NLT]). Once the devil has a foot in the door, it is only a matter of time, before the devil begins to rip your marital bond apart.

- ✓ **Tip 8: Keep Christ at the Center of Your Marriage and Pray With Your Spouse**

So they are no longer two, but one flesh. Therefore what God has joined together, let no one separate. (Matthew 19:6 [NIV])

In all thy ways acknowledge him, and he shall direct thy paths. (Proverbs 3:6 [KJV])

If any of you lacks wisdom, you should ask God, who gives generously to all without finding fault, and it will be given to you. (James 1:5 [NIV])

Put God first in your marriage and everything else will fall into place. After all, God intends for you to stay happily married. And, because marriage is a spiritual relationship, it is necessary for you and your spouse to have an individual relationship with God. Therefore, obey God through scripture and prayer individually and as a couple, and you will have a successful marriage, as God's Word is the cure for restoring love and happiness.

Embracing, believing, and acting on God's plan can remove the bitterness, resentment, brokenness, and disappointments in your marriage. Praying with your spouse and for your spouse invites God's power in to restore your marriage. However, going before God in prayer does not mean your marriage will always be "peaches and cream," but what it does mean is that through the Holy Spirit, you will be better equipped to handle conflicts, because you will have the same power that raised Jesus from the dead in your marriage. *So pray!* Pray with and for your spouse for wisdom, problem-solving, strength, forgiveness, and most importantly, unconditional love for each other.

✓ **Tip 9: Discuss Financial Matters**

And if a house is divided against itself, that house cannot stand. (Mark 3:25 [KJV])

Finances between you and your spouse should be decided together. When you become married, possessions and finances become "ours" instead of "mine" and "yours." As individuals, we tend to overlook this concept, thus, causing disagreements over finances. *So, make financial decisions with your spouse.*

If your spouse does not work outside of the home, do not hold that against him or her. Instead, work together to create a budget that works for you both. You and your spouse should have an equal amount (whenever possible) to spend, without providing justification for what you spend.

Refrain from hiding purchases from your spouse, and keeping financial secrets from him or her. Of course, managing finances together may not be easy, because it reveals what is important to you and your spouse. However, setting financial priorities with regard to debt, savings, expenses, and so on will help you and your spouse decrease the total number of disagreements you have.

✓ Tip 10: Talk About Your Intimacy Needs

Marriage should be honored by all, and the marriage bed should be kept pure… (Hebrews 13:4 [NIV])

Therefore shall a man leave his father and his mother, and shall cleave unto his wife: and they shall become one flesh. (Genesis 2:24 [KJV])

Being intimate with your spouse is a way to celebrate oneness in the sight of God. Intimacy in your marriage was created to be gratifying, passionate, and pleasurable. Therefore, you must understand your spouse's wants and needs. To do this, a conversation with your spouse about likes and dislikes between the sheets is necessary. Remember, your spouse is not a mind reader, but he or she most likely wants to please you in the bedroom. So, it is your responsibility to let him or her know how to do a great job. Don't forget that intimacy is not just physical.

In fact, true intimacy is built on commitment, passion, companionship, and spirituality. Embedded in these four factors, you will find faithfulness, respect, forgiveness, planning, creativity, communication, tenderness, spending time together, prayer, and the Word of God. This means you have to have a balance of all four factors to have a healthy marriage. It is very difficult to have a healthy relationship without being intimate. Therefore, whatever issue you and your spouse are grappling with, in regards to intimacy, you need to grow your love, God's way, in order to fix it.

✓ **Tip 11: Keep Your Issues in Your Marriage**

> *Give all your worries and cares to God, for he cares about you. (1 Peter 5:7 [NLT])*

> *Give your burdens to the LORD, and he will take care of you. He will not permit the Godly to slip and fall. (Psalm 55:22 [NLT])*

Your marital problems should not be shared with everyone. Even if you do have a close relationship with your parents, other family members, and friends, it is not healthy to tell them about everything going on in your marriage. I know sometimes you may need to vent, but when these times arise, seek God's guidance and help from your Pastor, minister, or marriage counselor.

After all, we are to cast all our cares onto God. He does not tell us to cast just some of our cares, but *all* of them. God has already laid out the plan for your marriage, so if it is to be successful, you have to make a decision to put God in your marriage, and not Mom, Dad, Uncle Jo-Jo, and everybody else.

These tips have helped me rebuild my marriage. Because, God does not show favoritism, (Acts 10:34) if you apply these tips to your marriage, you will be on the right path to rebuilding it. Again, there is no one-size-fits-all plan for obtaining a happy and healthy marriage; however, there is only one path. God's path. God's plan will help you and your spouse overcome issues together, serve each other, and most importantly serve God.

Yes, it is possible to overcome issues and grow your love God's way, once you decide to speak your truth. Vocalizing your truth is the hardest part, but it is an essential step that cannot be ignored, if you are committed to your decision to love your spouse no matter what. The steps you and your spouse take to grow and sustain your love may be different from others, but if you and your spouse work towards following the principles outlined in the Word for marriage and use these tips, your marriage will be successful.

If you enjoyed this book, you will enjoy the *Growing Your Love After The "I Do's" God's Way Workbook*. The workbook is designed to be a companion to this book so you can reap the maximum benefits of this book.

Sign up at http://eepurl.com/cNLi5z to get information on pre-orders and discounts for the *Growing Your Love After The "I Do's" God's Way Workbook* when it is released August 2017.

www.ingramcontent.com/pod-product-compliance
Lightning Source LLC
Chambersburg PA
CBHW070631300426
44113CB00010B/1731